Taking Tests

Contents

LESSON 1	Preparing for Tests	2
LESSON 2	Studying for Tests	6
LESSON 3	Understanding Test Directions	10
LESSON 4	Answering Multiple-Choice Questions	14
LESSON 5	Answering Matching Questions	18
LESSON 6	Answering True-False Questions	20
LESSON 7	Answering Short-Answer Questions	22
LESSON 8	Writing Complete-Sentence Answers	24
LESSON 9	Taking Tests	28
REVIEW	Preparing for Tests	30
REVIEW	Taking Different Kinds of Tests	31
ANSWER KEY		Inside Back Cover

Acknowledgments

Executive Editor: Diane Sharpe
Supervising Editor: Stephanie Muller
Design Manager: Laura Cole
Cover Designer: D. Childress/Alan Klemp

Product Development: Curriculum Concepts, Inc.
Writer: Steven L. Stern

Illustrators: pp. 21, 23 top Janet Bohn; pp. 4, 28 Toby Gowing; pp. 14, 25, 27 Al Hering; pp. 7, 12, 16 Michael McDermott; p. 2 Tom Sperling; pp. 11, 23 bottom Steve Stankiewicz
Photography: cover © CE Nagele/FPG

ISBN 0-8114-2529-0

Copyright © 1994 Steck-Vaughn Company.
All rights reserved. No part of the material protected by this copyright may be reproduced or utilized in any form or by any means, electronic or mechanical, including photocopying, recording, or by any information storage and retrieval system, without permission in writing from the copyright owner. Requests for permission to make copies of any part of the work should be mailed to: Copyright Permissions, Steck-Vaughn Company, P.O. Box 26015, Austin, TX 78755. Printed in the United States of America.

1 2 3 4 5 6 7 8 9 0 CCG 00 99 98 97 96 95 94

LESSON 1: Preparing for Tests

To do well on tests, it is important to plan ahead. Think about the material that will be covered on the test. Then decide how best to study and how to use your time wisely.

Ask Yourself

Do you think you have good study habits? Beside each statement, write <u>usually</u>, <u>sometimes</u>, or <u>never</u>. Then follow the scoring instructions.

1. For big tests, I do all my studying the night before._____
2. I study while watching television._____
3. I'm too busy with other activities to study for tests._____
4. I forget the dates of upcoming tests._____
5. I don't understand the material I'm studying._____
6. I get interrupted while I'm studying._____
7. I don't study all the material I should for a test._____
8. I spend too much time studying the wrong things._____
9. I forget books or papers that I need to study._____
10. I let my mind wander when I should be studying._____

SCORING: For every <u>never</u> answer, give yourself four points. For every <u>sometimes</u> answer, give yourself two points. Score no points for <u>usually</u> answers.

If you scored 30 or more points, you can be proud of your study habits. If you scored 18–28 points, your study habits could improve. If you scored 16 or fewer points, you need to get serious about studying.

2

How To

Plan for a Test

- Find out exactly what material the test will cover.
- Be certain you know the test date. Write it down.
- Don't put off getting help. If there is something you don't understand, ask for help <u>before</u> it's time to begin studying.
- Bring home the books, notes, and papers you will need to study.
- Don't try to study too much in one day. Spread study time over several days. If you have much to cover, do your studying over a week or more.
- For large tests, make a written study schedule. Plan which days you will study and for how long.
- Start studying early, and allow plenty of time. It's better to find that you have left too much time rather than too little.
- Give yourself extra time for review on the day before the test.

Try It Out

Read about each situation. Explain how you should plan for the test. Look at the **How To** box for hints.

1. You have a social studies test in one week. The test will cover Chapters 7–11. You know Chapters 7, 8, 9, and 10 well. Because you were sick, you haven't even read Chapter 11 yet.

2. Today is Monday. You have a science test Wednesday. You won't have much time to study on Tuesday because you're going to a special program at the library. Also, you're not sure exactly what the test will cover.

3. In two weeks, you have a math test that will cover everything you've learned in the past two months. There's so much material to review that you don't know where to begin.

How To

Prepare to Study

- Gather the books, notes, and papers you need.
- Choose a quiet study place with good light, where you won't be interrupted.
- Think about the kind of test it will be and how you can best study for it. For some tests, you need to understand ideas or memorize facts. Other tests require you to practice such skills as adding fractions or creating a well-written paragraph.
- Know your strengths and weaknesses. Concentrate your study time on the material that you need to study the most.
- Decide whether it would help to spend time studying with another person. Usually you should study by yourself. However, you may find it useful to review with someone else after you have studied alone.

Try It Out

Read each student's study plan. Tell whether it is good or how you would improve it. Look at the *How To* box for hints.

1. There is an important English test tomorrow. Jackie and her friend Shana plan to study together. Last week, they were supposed to study together for a science test, but all they did was watch TV. Neither of them did well on that test.

   _____
   _____
   _____
   _____
   _____
   _____

4

2. Thomas is preparing for a social studies test. He has four chapters to study. He plans to study three of them but skip the fourth because he thinks that chapter is boring.

_____
_____

3. Diane has a test on fractions and decimals this week. She knows fractions very well but still feels uncertain about some decimal problems. She is spending most of her study time on fractions.

_____
_____

4. Burt has to study for a test, but his friend invites him to watch a ball game on TV. Burt decides to take his textbook to his friend's house and study while he's watching the game.

_____
_____

5. Today is Thursday. Next Monday Letty will have a social studies test. On Tuesday, there will be an English test. Letty's family is planning a party for her grandmother's birthday this Sunday, so Letty is going to study for the social studies test tomorrow. Then she will help with the party. On Monday, she will study for the English test.

_____
_____

What Have I Learned?

Suppose you are making a study chart. Add suggestions to the chart below.

PREPARING FOR A TEST

DO	DON'T
Know what the test will cover.	Wait until the night before to study.
_____	_____
_____	_____
_____	_____

5

LESSON 2
Studying for Tests

The way you study for a test is as important as the actual material you study. Using a good study system will help you learn and remember material. The **READ-TEST-CHECK** method will make studying easier and more effective.

Ask Yourself

Are some materials harder to learn than others? Read each item below. Then write a number from 1 to 5 to rate how easy or hard each item is to learn. In your rating, use 1 for easiest, 5 for hardest, and 3 for average.

1. how to use commas correctly _____
2. the meanings of vocabulary words _____
3. working with decimals or fractions _____
4. how to read a graph _____
5. historical facts _____
6. how to spell words _____
7. how to write a topic sentence _____
8. scientific explanations _____
9. mathematical problem-solving methods _____
10. how to read a map _____
11. rules of grammar _____
12. how to find the main idea in a paragraph _____

Circle the items for which you wrote either 4 or 5. Some of these items will become easier for you with practice using the **READ-TEST-CHECK** study method.

How To

Use the READ-TEST-CHECK Study Method

- **Read** the material or say it to yourself until you think you know it. Study a small portion of the material at a time.
- **Test** yourself. Try to remember or repeat the information without looking at it.
- **Check** to see if you remembered the information correctly. If not, READ-TEST-CHECK again.
- When you can remember the information correctly, study the next section.

Try It Out

Use the READ-TEST-CHECK method to study the article below. Then cover the article with a sheet of paper, and answer the questions that follow. If you have trouble, use READ-TEST-CHECK again.

Birds of Prey

Birds that hunt and eat animals are called **birds of prey**. They include hawks, falcons, and vultures. All birds of prey have sharp, hooked beaks and long claws, or **talons**, which they use for catching and killing their prey.

The hawks include eagles, harriers, kites, and the fish-eating osprey. One of the largest eagles is the monkey-eating eagle of the Philippines.

The falcons are fast-flying hunters. They dive at their prey. The peregrine falcon can spot its prey half a mile away and dive at nearly 180 miles an hour.

Vultures are birds of prey that eat dead animals. They have no feathers on their heads.

1. What is a bird of prey?
   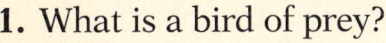
   _____

2. Describe how birds of prey look.
   _____
   _____

3. Name three examples of birds of prey.
   _____
   _____

4. What do vultures eat?
   _____
   _____

How To

Study for Tests

- To learn information in a paragraph, take notes as you read. Writing down key facts will help you understand and remember.
- If you find it hard to remember an idea, try expressing it in a different way, using your own words.
- Some tests require you to demonstrate your ability to do something, such as subtracting decimals or punctuating sentences. Use READ-TEST-CHECK to learn the rules. Then use your study time to practice. Review examples from class notes, homework assignments, and earlier tests.
- Give yourself time to review the material thoroughly. If you forget anything, use READ-TEST-CHECK to relearn it.
- Use READ-TEST-CHECK to work with a friend. After you both study the material, check each other.

Try It Out

Use READ-TEST-CHECK to study the time line and chart below. Then cover the time line and chart with a sheet of paper. Answer the questions on the following page. If you have trouble, use READ-TEST-CHECK again.

EXPLORERS OF NORTH AMERICA

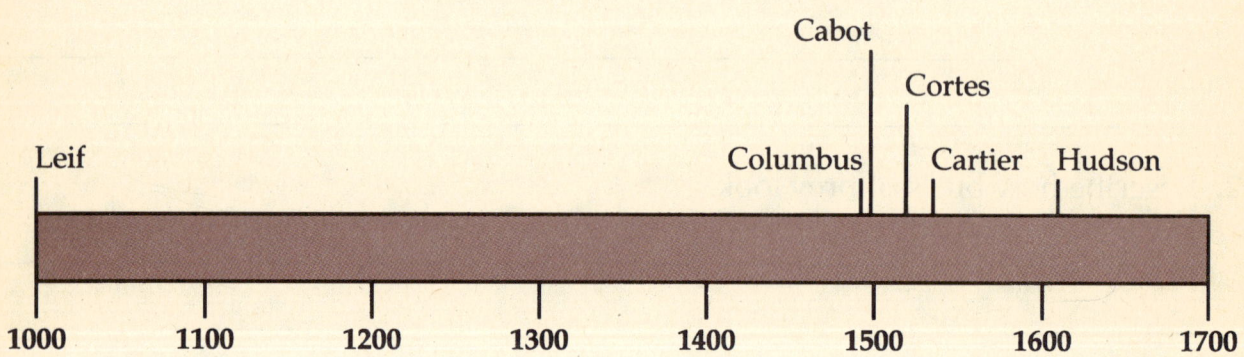

Explorer	Date of Trip	Country Sent By
Leif	1000	Norway
Columbus	1492	Spain
Cabot	1497	England
de Leon	1513	Spain
Cortes	1519	Spain

Explorer	Date of Trip	Country Sent By
de Vaca & Esteban	1528	Spain
Cartier	1535	France
Coronado	1541	Spain
Champlain	1608	France
Hudson	1609	Netherlands

1. Who is the first explorer listed on the chart and the time line?

2. The chart lists eleven explorers involved in ten trips. What country sent two explorers in 1528?

3. How many of the explorers listed on the chart are not shown on the time line?

4. Of the ten trips listed in the chart, half of them were sponsored by one country. What is the name of that country?

5. Three countries each sponsored only one of the trips listed on the chart. What are the names of each country?

6. During what century were most of the trips taken?

7. Approximately how many years elapsed between Leif's trip for Norway and Columbus's trip for Spain?

8. Who is the last explorer listed on the chart and the time line?

What Have I Learned?

Suppose you were taking a test that covered the first three chapters in your science textbook. Explain how you could use the information you learned in this lesson to help you study. Give examples.

9

Understanding Test Directions

When taking a test, it is essential to understand the directions fully. Read them carefully, and think about what you need to do. Do not begin to write until you are sure you understand the directions.

Ask Yourself

Read each example. First, describe the problem you think the student may have. Then suggest how the student can avoid the problem in the future.

1. Kenny is answering an essay question on a social studies test. His answer is well-written. However, because he read the directions too quickly, he is answering only half the question.

   PROBLEM:_____

   SUGGESTION: _____

2. Sheila is taking an end-of-unit math test. To save time, she just glances at the directions before going right to work.

   PROBLEM:_____

   SUGGESTION: _____

3. Christine is confused about the meaning of an essay question on an English test. She doesn't want to bother the teacher, so she starts writing.

   PROBLEM:_____

   SUGGESTION: _____

4. The directions for Ethan's science test read: "Write true if the sentence is true. If the sentence is false, rewrite it to make it true." Ethan reads just the first sentence of the directions and then skips to the questions and starts writing true or false beside each sentence.

   PROBLEM:_____

   SUGGESTION: _____

How do you think these students' grades were affected by the ways in which they answered their test questions?

How To

Understand Test Directions

Read the directions carefully once or twice. Ask yourself:
- What type of test questions am I answering?
- Does the test contain more than one kind of question?
- How should I write my answers? Where should I write them?
- Do I have to write in complete sentences?
- Do I need to look at a graph, map, table, or picture?
- Watch for key words that tell you what to do, especially such verbs as: *read, write, circle, underline, choose, solve, use, compare, describe, estimate, explain,* and *include.*
- Read each question with care. Think about what task you are being asked to do and what information you are supposed to give.
- Watch for questions that ask for more than one piece of information or that ask you to do more than one task. Answer each question completely.
- Ask for help if you are uncertain about what to do.

Try It Out

Read each set of directions, and answer the questions that follow. Circle the letter of the best answer.

> **DIRECTIONS:** Use the information given in the bar graph to make a table.

1. Which key words tell you what to do?
   a. use, make
   b. table, make
   c. use, information
   d. use, table

2. To answer this question, you have to
   a. write a complete sentence.
   b. draw a picture.
   c. make a table.
   d. make a bar graph.

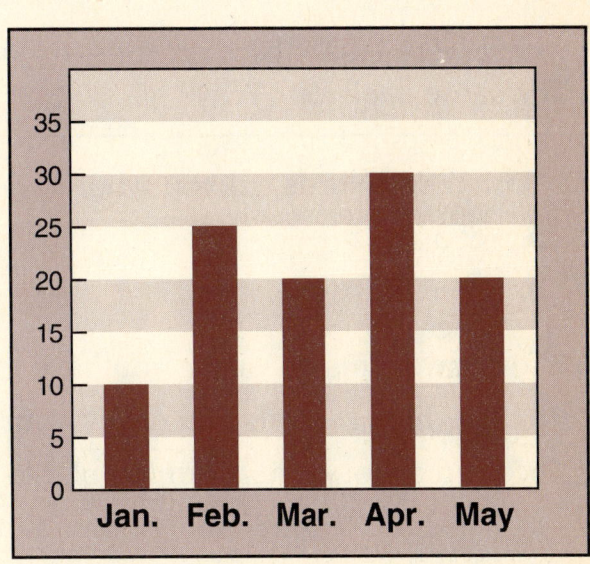

11

> **DIRECTIONS:** Look at the map on this page. Circle the names of the battles on the map. Were most Civil War battles fought in the North or in the South? Write your answer on the line.

3. Which key words tell you what to do?
   - **a.** look, fought
   - **b.** look, circle
   - **c.** look, circle, write
   - **d.** circle, look, fought

4. To answer this question, you have to
   - **a.** do three tasks.
   - **b.** write a paragraph.
   - **c.** draw a map.
   - **d.** read a paragraph.

> **DIRECTIONS:** Read the story, and answer the question below. Write in complete sentences. Proofread your work.
>
> What were Lisa's three reasons for joining the team? Would you have made the same decision? Why?

5. Which key words tell you what to do?
   - **a.** read
   - **b.** write, answer
   - **c.** proofread
   - **d.** all of the above

6. To answer this question, you have to
   - **a.** list three reasons and check your work.
   - **b.** read a story and fill in the blanks.
   - **c.** list three reasons and answer a question.
   - **d.** read a story and answer three connected questions.

> **DIRECTIONS:** Solve by finding the pattern. Write the rule. Then answer the question.
>
> What is the next number in the pattern?
> 2, 6, 18, . . .

7. Which key words tell you what to do?

    a. solve, number

    b. solve, write, question

    c. solve, write, answer

    d. write, answer

8. To answer this question, you have to

    a. do one task.

    b. do three tasks.

    c. do two tasks.

    d. do four tasks.

> **DIRECTIONS:** Read the article, and study the drawings. Write one or two paragraphs that compare a spider's home with one of the other homes shown. Explain how they are alike and how they are different. Consider the shapes of the homes, the building materials used to create them, and the purpose for each home.

9. Which group of key words tells you everything you need to do?

    a. read, study

    b. article, drawings

    c. consider

    d. none of the above

10. To answer this question, you have to

    a. write at least one paragraph and draw a picture.

    b. look at pictures and read an article before writing.

    c. explain how spiders build their homes.

    d. describe the shape of spiders.

What Have I Learned?

Review some of your old test papers. Did you do everything suggested in this lesson's *How To* box? Tell which rules you followed and what you would do differently now.

_____

_____

_____

LESSON 4
Answering Multiple-Choice Questions

There are several different kinds of test questions. One common type is multiple choice. Multiple-choice questions require you to choose from several possible answers. Always read and consider all the choices before deciding on an answer.

Ask Yourself

How much do you know about answering multiple-choice questions? Read each statement below. If you think the statement is correct, write <u>agree</u>. If you think the statement is wrong, write <u>disagree</u>.

1. To answer some multiple-choice questions, you may need to study a graph or map._____

2. To save time, it's smart to choose the first answer you read that seems correct._____

3. It's wise to read just the first sentence of the directions and then get right to work._____

4. The directions for a multiple-choice test always require you to write the letter of your choice on a line._____

5. "All of the above" means that all of the other answer choices are correct._____

If you wrote <u>agree</u> only for numbers 1 and 5, you understand the basic guidelines for taking a multiple-choice test.

How To

Answer Multiple-Choice Questions

- Read the directions. Be sure you understand them before you begin. You may have to mark each answer by circling a choice, writing a letter on a line, or darkening a circle for the answer you choose.
- Read each question carefully.
- Study tables, graphs, maps, photographs, illustrations, or pictures before answering questions. Be sure you understand the information presented.
- In some tests you read a paragraph and then answer questions. It may help to skim the questions before you read the paragraph.
- Read all the choices that are given. Consider each one.
- Choose <u>all of the above</u> only if every other choice is correct. Choose <u>none of the above</u> only if every other choice is wrong.
- If you are unsure of the answer, cross out choices you know are wrong.
- Don't spend too much time on a difficult question. Narrow your choices and make your best guess. If you have time, return to that question after you have answered all the others.
- If you are answering questions about a reading selection, look back in the selection to find the answer.
- Choose the best answer.

Try It Out

Answer the multiple-choice questions.

A. Write the letter of the correct answer on the blank before the question.

_____ 1. Which sentence is true?

    a. A nickel is 1/3 of a dime.   **c.** A penny is 1/4 of a dime.

    b. A quarter is 1/2 of a dollar.   **d.** None of the above is true.

_____ 2. What fraction of the circle has light shading?

    a. 3/4   **c.** 1/2

    b. 1/4   **d.** 2/3

_____ 3. What fraction of the circle has dark shading?

    a. 1/2   **c.** 1/4

    b. 1/3   **d.** 1/8

B. Darken the circle for the sentence that is written correctly.

1. **A** Tracie was practicing for the band.
   B Jane and I am going to a movie.
   C Will them give us a ride home?
   D We heard him was in the play.

2. **F** The city was builded in 1660.
   G Yesterday we will tour the castle.
   H A silk scarf in the market.
   J Our hotel is near the river.

3. **A** The baby coughed and cried loud.
   B Did you call the doctor?
   C The baby was serious ill.
   D Father gentle rocked the baby.

4. **F** The cows were near the creek.
   G We seen many farms today.
   H The farmers has plowed their fields.
   J There weren't no crops growing.

1. Ⓐ Ⓑ Ⓒ Ⓓ
2. Ⓕ Ⓖ Ⓗ Ⓙ
3. Ⓐ Ⓑ Ⓒ Ⓓ
4. Ⓕ Ⓖ Ⓗ Ⓙ

C. Read the passage. Circle the letter for the correct answer.

Scientists have learned some interesting facts about a bird called an albatross. The albatross is a large, white bird that eats fish it catches in the ocean. An albatross has a wing span of about eleven feet. That means the distance from the tip of one wing to the tip of the other, when the bird's wings are spread, is eleven feet.

These birds lay their eggs in nests that they build on islands near the South Pole. Often there is only one egg, and the father and mother bird take turns sitting on it.

One albatross will sit on an egg for about two months while the other bird hunts for fish. The bird on the nest does not eat at all. The other bird flies over the ocean looking for and catching fish. The bird that is hunting may fly hundreds of miles a day searching for food. Before it returns home to take its turn protecting the nest, it may have flown as many as eight thousand miles!

1. This story is mainly about
   a. catching fish.
   b. the albatross.
   c. hatching eggs.
   d. flying over the ocean.
2. Where does the albatross like to build its nest?
   a. on islands
   b. in the sea
   c. on mountains
   d. on rocky cliffs
3. The distance from the tip of one wing to the tip of the other wing is called the
   a. wing span.
   b. flight range.
   c. nest.
   d. none of the above
4. An albatross sitting on a nest may go without food for as long as
   a. one year.
   b. six months.
   c. two months.
   d. three weeks.
5. When one albatross sits on a nest, the other one usually
   a. makes strange sounds.
   b. hunts.
   c. builds another nest.
   d. all of the above
6. Why does one albatross always stay with the nest?
   a. It is not hungry.
   b. It is tired.
   c. It is protecting the nest.
   d. It doesn't like to fly.
7. How many miles might an albatross fly before it returns to the nest?
   a. 100 miles
   b. 800 miles
   c. 8,000 miles
   d. 1,000 miles
8. What does the albatross do while it is flying?
   a. It looks for food.
   b. It protects the nest.
   c. It fights enemies.
   d. It makes strange sounds.

What Have I Learned?

Why is it important to read all the choices on a multiple-choice test before choosing one?

_____
_____
_____
_____

LESSON 5
Answering Matching Questions

A matching test is similar to a multiple-choice test, but there are many more answers from which to choose. On a matching test, carefully read all the answer choices for each item, and then make the best match.

Ask Yourself

Are you familiar with matching tests? Match each item in the first column with its definition in the second column. Then write the letter of the matching item in the space.

_____ 1. George Washington   a. a country in Asia

_____ 2. Alaska   b. first U.S. President

_____ 3. elephant   c. largest living land animal

_____ 4. India   d. the planet nearest to the sun

_____ 5. the Pacific Ocean   e. the largest U.S. state

_____ 6. Mercury   f. the world's largest ocean

Did you have to guess at any of the answers? Would it be easier to make a guess before you matched most of the other items, or after you matched most of them?

How To

Answer Matching Questions

- Read the directions. Be sure you understand them.
- Read the first item in the left-hand column.
- Read <u>all</u> the choices in the right-hand column.
- Choose the best answer.
- If you are not sure of an answer, skip the item and return to it later. You will have fewer choices left to match.
- When one column has more items than the other column, you will have some choices left after matching all the items in the first column.

18

Try It Out

Match each item in Column A with an item from Column B. Write the letter of your answer in the space beside the number. Look at the **How To** box for hints. If you need help, use a reference book.

A

_____ 1. war that the United States fought to gain independence from Britain

_____ 2. large province in Canada

_____ 3. President of the U.S. during the Civil War

_____ 4. war between the North and the South in the United States, 1861–1865

_____ 5. first woman to pilot an airplane across the Atlantic Ocean

_____ 6. communication system that uses Morse code

_____ 7. wide, level stretch of grassland east of the Rocky Mountains

_____ 8. ship that can travel deep under water

_____ 9. longest river in the U.S.

_____ 10. transportation system that linked eastern and western United States

_____ 11. largest country in South America

_____ 12. Native Americans of the northern plains

B

a. Brazil
b. George Washington Carver
c. transcontinental railroad
d. telegraph
e. Abraham Lincoln
f. Civil War
g. Amelia Earhart
h. Ontario
i. Japan
j. Great Plains
k. submarine
l. Sioux
m. Mississippi River
n. Revolutionary War

What Have I Learned?

In what ways are tests with matching questions the same as tests with multiple-choice questions? In what ways are they different?

_____
_____
_____
_____

Answering True-False Questions

True-false questions on a test can be tricky. Read each statement carefully and completely. Then think about the exact meaning of each statement before you write your answer.

Ask Yourself

Have you taken a test that had tricky true-false questions? Write <u>true</u> in the blank if the statement is true. Write <u>false</u> if it is false.

_____ 1. The sun is larger than the moon.

_____ 2. The sun is smaller than Earth.

_____ 3. The sun is larger than the moon but smaller than Earth.

What can you conclude from answering the three questions? If part of a statement is false, the entire statement is _____.

How To

Answer True-False Questions

- Read the directions. Be sure you understand them.
- Read each statement two or three times. Think about the meaning of the statement. Then decide if it is true or false.
- Remember that if any part of a statement is false, the entire statement is false.
- Certain words can make a true statement false or a false statement true. Watch for these words:

    | all | never | often |
    | always | no | sometimes |
    | every | not | usually |

- Some tests require that you rewrite false statements so they are true. For example, the false statement "All planets in our solar system have at least one moon" may be restated correctly as "Not all planets in our solar system have moons."

20

Try It Out

Read the passage and the statements that follow. Write T if the statement is true. Write F if it is false. Look at the **How To** box for hints.

Robots can perform many different jobs. They paint automobiles. They put machines together. They handle poisons. Most of the tasks that robots carry out are too dangerous or unpleasant for people to do. By carrying out such tasks, robots serve as workers' helpers.

Few robots look anything like people. They are machines. Like other pieces of machinery, they come in different shapes and sizes. The way they are built depends on the jobs they do. Most robots have a single arm that can lift things. Most are built to handle tools.

Each robot has a computer inside it. Skilled technicians program instructions for the computer. The computer tells the robot what to do.

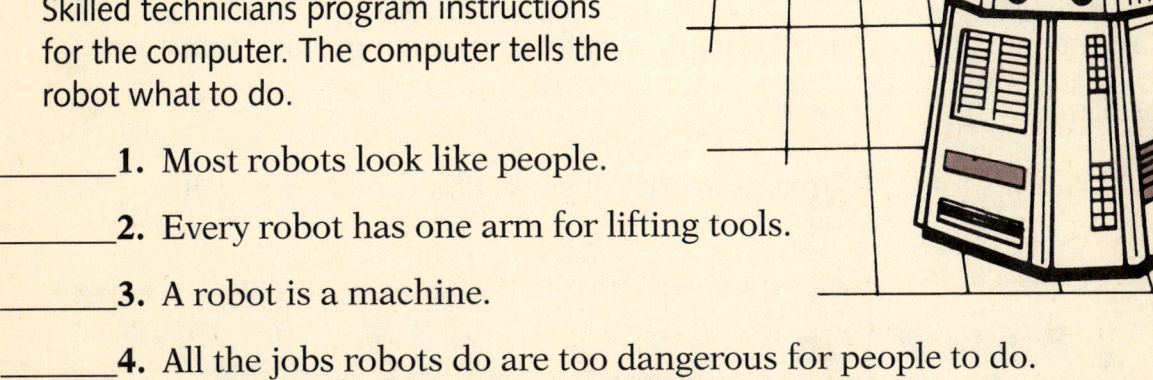

_____ 1. Most robots look like people.

_____ 2. Every robot has one arm for lifting tools.

_____ 3. A robot is a machine.

_____ 4. All the jobs robots do are too dangerous for people to do.

_____ 5. Robots are able to do various kinds of tasks.

_____ 6. Workers serve as robots' helpers.

_____ 7. Robots have built-in computers, which they program themselves.

_____ 8. Robots are built differently for different jobs.

What Have I Learned?

Review the numbered statements in *Try It Out*. On your own paper, rewrite each false sentence to make it true.

21

LESSON 7
Answering Short-Answer Questions

Fill-in-the-blank and other short-answer questions usually require you to write one or more words on a blank line. Sometimes your answer completes a sentence. Other times your answer is the solution to a problem or the answer to a question about a map, a graph, or a chapter you have read.

Ask Yourself

Do you find short-answer questions challenging? Read each statement below. Write yes if the statement is true for you. Write no if it isn't.

1. I always read instructions carefully before I begin._____

2. I read the entire sentence before trying to answer a fill-in-the-blank question._____

3. I look at surrounding words for clues to help me find the answer._____

4. I plan the facts or numbers to include before answering a short-answer question._____

Did you write yes for all four statements? If so, you're doing very well!

How To

Answer Short-Answer Questions

- Read the directions. Be sure you understand them.
- For fill-in-the-blank questions:
    Carefully read the entire sentence.
    Look for context clues in surrounding words.
    Fill in the word that makes the most sense.
    Reread the sentence to check your answer.
- For other short-answer questions:
    Read the entire question or problem carefully.
    Think before you write. Decide what information your answer must include.

Try It Out

A. Read the passage. Write the word or words that best complete each sentence.

When the moon moves between the sun and Earth, the sun's rays are cut off and the sky grows dark. This is called a **solar eclipse.** An eclipse may be total (when little light gets through) or partial. In a total eclipse, the sun's flaring outer atmosphere, the **corona,** is visible.

A **lunar eclipse** takes place when Earth moves between the sun and the moon, and the moon is in Earth's shadow. The sun's rays no longer shine on the moon, and it appears to grow dim.

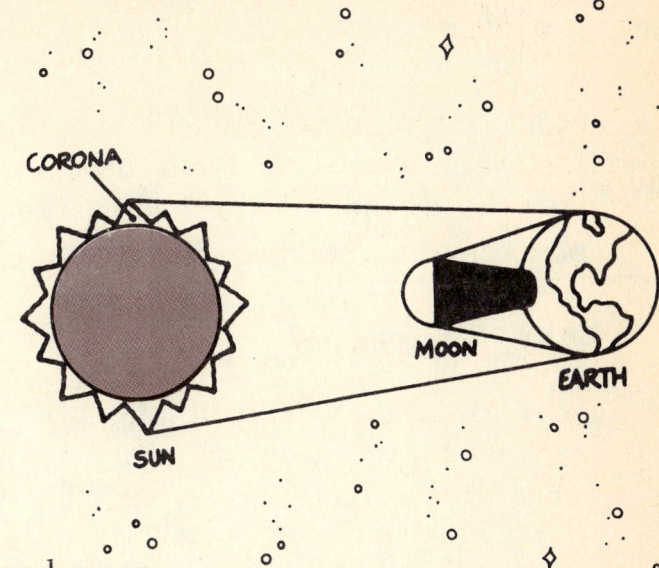

1. When Earth passes between the sun and moon, it causes a _____.

2. In a solar eclipse, the moon blocks the sun's _____.

3. The outer atmosphere of the sun that is seen during an eclipse is called the _____.

4. During a lunar eclipse, the _____ seems to grow dim because the _____ is no longer shining on it.

B. Use the map to answer the questions. You do not have to answer in complete sentences.

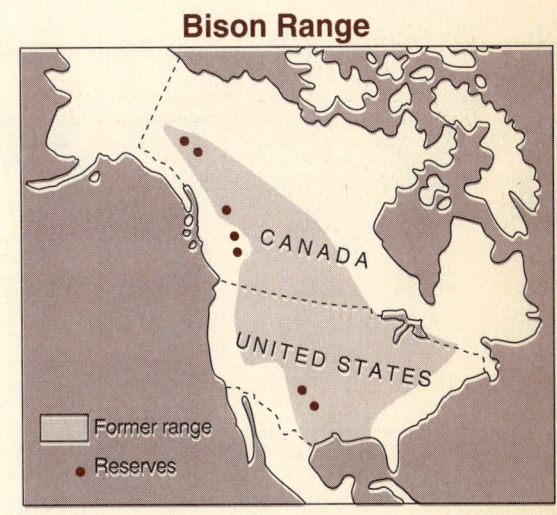

1. What two countries are shown as areas where bison once roamed?
   _____

2. Which country has some bison reserves that are <u>outside</u> the former ranging areas of bison? _____

3. How many bison reserves are located in the United States? _____

What Have I Learned?

What **How To** tips for short-answer questions could also help you answer true-false or matching questions? Tell why on your own paper.

Lesson 8: Writing Complete-Sentence Answers

Some tests require that you answer questions by writing complete sentences. Essay questions require you to write a complete paragraph. Decide on the information that must be included to answer a question. It is important to plan sentences and paragraphs before you write them.

Ask Yourself

Why do you think it is important to plan ahead when you answer an essay question? If you were writing a paragraph to answer each question below, what ideas or facts would you include?

1. Why is it important to get a good education?

    IDEAS: _____
    _____
    _____
    _____

2. Describe the bravest thing you ever did.

    IDEAS: _____
    _____
    _____
    _____

3. Think of a book that you enjoyed reading. What two qualities did you like in the main character? Why did you like them?

    IDEAS: _____
    _____
    _____
    _____

How is answering an essay question like writing a composition or report?

How To

Write Complete-Sentence Answers

- Read the directions. Be sure you understand them.
- Read the question carefully.
- Plan your answer. Choose the main idea or ideas.
- Jot down facts or details that support your answer.
- Include only information that relates to your topic.
- Change the question into part of the answer. For example, change "Why did the Roman Empire fall?" into "The Roman Empire fell because. . . ." Or, change the question into a topic sentence: "The Roman Empire fell for three reasons. First, . . ."
- If you are writing a paragraph, begin it with a topic sentence.
- When you finish writing, reread your answer. Be sure you have answered the question clearly and completely.
- Check spelling, capitalization, and punctuation.

Try It Out

A. Read the article below. Use complete sentences to answer the questions on the next page.

Neon

Many brightly colored lights are made from a gas called neon. Neon is one of many gases in the air. About eighty years ago, a French chemist found a way to use neon to make lights. He took the air out of a glass tube. Then he replaced it with neon. When electricity was passed through the neon, it created a colorful light.

Signs using neon lights are visible along many highways. Airports sometimes use neon lights to guide airplanes because neon can be seen through thick fog. Some people use neon signs in their businesses and offices. Some works of art are made of neon lights.

Some signs use other gases. Argon is another gas used in signs. It gives off a lavender color. Neon gives off an orange-red color. Even though different gases may be used, people always call the signs "neon" signs.

25

1. What is neon?

   _____

   _____

2. When was neon first used to make lights?

   _____

   _____

3. How is neon used to make lights?

   _____

   _____

4. Why do some airports use neon lights?

   _____

   _____

5. Besides airports, give two other examples of how neon is used.

   _____

   _____

6. How is argon different from neon?

   _____

   _____

B. Review your answers to questions 1–5 above. Then answer the questions below.

1. Are your answers clear and complete? _____ If not, what can you do

   about it? _____

2. Have you written complete sentences? _____ If not, how can you

   complete them? _____

3. Do your sentences start with a capital letter and end with a period? _____
   If not, go back to the answers and make the necessary changes.

4. Are all of your words spelled correctly? _____ If not, go back to the article
   and find the correct spelling for any words you misspelled. Now go back to
   your answers and make the necessary spelling corrections.

C. Answer each question by writing a paragraph. On your own paper, jot down ideas, facts, or details you plan to include. Then, begin your paragraph with a topic sentence.

1. What is the most important thing in life? Money? Fame? Friendship? Power? Something else? Give two or more reasons for your answer.

_____
_____
_____
_____
_____

2. School should continue twelve months a year. Do you agree or disagree with this statement? Explain why. Support your opinion with at least three clearly stated reasons.

_____
_____
_____
_____
_____
_____

What Have I Learned?

Suppose you wrote the answers to Exercise C in *Try It Out* without planning them first. What might have gone wrong?

_____
_____

27

LESSON 9
Taking Tests

To do your best on a test, prepare well and use your time wisely. The better prepared you are, the easier the test will seem. Always double-check your answers when you finish.

Ask Yourself

How good are your test-taking skills? Complete each sentence by darkening the circle of the answer that best describes you.

1. When I take a test, I usually
   - Ⓐ have more time than I need.
   - Ⓑ don't have enough time to finish.
   - Ⓒ have just the right amount of time.

2. Test directions
   - Ⓐ are often very confusing to me.
   - Ⓑ are easy for me to follow if I read them.
   - Ⓒ are so simple that I just skim them.

3. When I answer essay questions,
   - Ⓐ I reread my answers to be sure they are complete.
   - Ⓑ I double-check my spelling, capitalization, and punctuation.
   - Ⓒ I do both A and B.

4. When I'm considering a hard question or problem,
   - Ⓐ I sometimes spend more time on it than I should.
   - Ⓑ I do the best I can within a reasonable amount of time.
   - Ⓒ I sometimes just guess instead of thinking it through.

1. A or C	**3.** C
2. B	**4.** B

Do your answers match those in the box? If not, you may need to improve your test-taking skills.

How To

Take a Test

- Get a good night's sleep before the test, and eat a good breakfast. Remember to bring the materials you need.
- Read directions carefully. If you're unsure about what to do, ask.
- Preview the test before you begin. Plan your time, allowing yourself extra time to work on parts that appear difficult.
- Read carefully. You may need to read some questions more than once.
- Don't spend too much time on any one question. If you get stuck on one question, mark it and return to it later.
- Answer all questions. If you don't know an answer, make your best guess.
- Save time to go back and check your answers when you finish.
- Pay special attention to complete-sentence and paragraph answers. Proofread spelling, capitalization, and punctuation.

Try It Out

Read each incorrect statement below. Then rewrite it to make it correct.

1. If you don't know the answer to a fill-in-the-blank, leave the space blank.

_____

2. If you can't solve a problem, keep trying no matter how long it takes.

_____

3. Previewing a test before you start to work will only waste time.

_____

4. Allow the same amount of time to work on each part of a test.

_____

What Have I Learned?

What do you find hardest about taking tests? What could you do to make taking tests easier for yourself?

_____

_____

REVIEW Preparing for Tests

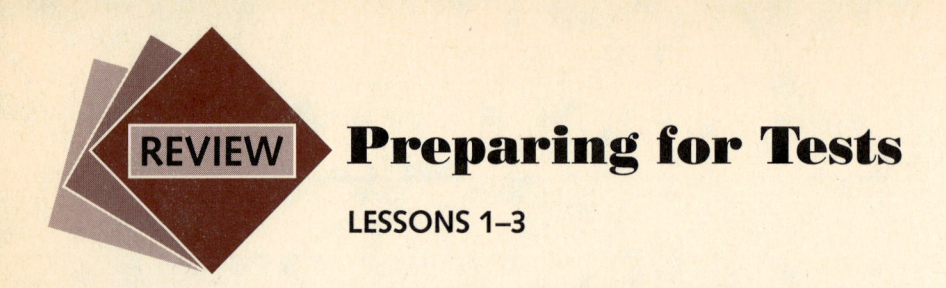

LESSONS 1–3

Reviewing What You Learned

Read each statement. Write <u>true</u> if it is true. If it is false, rewrite each statement to make it true.

1. You could use the READ-TEST-CHECK method to memorize a famous quotation.
   _____

2. To learn information in a paragraph, you should take notes as you read.
   _____

3. To prepare for a big test, do all your studying in one day.
   _____

4. It's wise to spend most of your test-preparation time studying the material you know well.
   _____
   _____

Using What You Know

Your teacher will write a paragraph on the board. Use the READ-TEST-CHECK method to learn the most important ideas in it. Then answer these questions.

1. What was the nickname of Mildred Didrikson Zaharias?
   _____

2. Name three sports that Mildred Zaharias was good at.
   _____

3. In what year did she compete in the Olympics?
   _____

4. What sport did she play for the greater part of her life?
   _____

REVIEW: Taking Different Kinds of Tests

LESSONS 4–9

Reviewing What You Learned

Write the phrase from the list that best completes each sentence. You will not use all the phrases for your answers.

1. Before you determine your answer for a multiple-choice or matching question, you should _____.

2. Words such as *always*, *never*, and *every* can _____.

3. The first thing to do when taking a test is to _____.

4. When taking a test with matching questions, you may sometimes _____.

5. To answer short-answer questions, you often need to _____.

6. To begin the answer to an essay question, you can _____.

7. Some tests require that you rewrite false statements _____.

---

answer only the questions you are sure of
read the directions and make sure you understand them
make a true statement false
write one or more words on a blank line
so they are true
change the question into a topic sentence
read and consider all the answer choices
use pen instead of pencil for writing answers
have items left over in one column

31

Using What You Know

A. Write two test-taking tips for each kind of test. Write in complete sentences. Be sure your answers are clear and complete.

1. **MULTIPLE-CHOICE TESTS:** _____
   _____
   _____

2. **MATCHING TESTS:** _____
   _____
   _____

3. **TRUE-FALSE TESTS:** _____
   _____
   _____

4. **SHORT-ANSWER TESTS:** _____
   _____
   _____

B. Answer the essay question below by writing one or more paragraphs. Plan your answer before you write. Begin with a topic sentence. If you need more space, use your own paper. Remember to check your spelling, capitalization, and punctuation.

There are certain things you can do that will help you do well on any kind of test. Name three of them, and explain why each one is so important.

_____
_____
_____
_____
_____
_____
_____